ADULTING IS A TRIP

Navigating Through the Journey of Adulthood

Ranada Dalton, LMHC, MAMFT, LPC
& Athena Salisbury

What's 4 U Publishing

Adulting is a Trip: Navigating Through the Journey of Adulthood

Copyright © 2021 Ranada Dalton and Athena Salisbury

All rights reserved. No part of this book may be reproduced or transmitted in any form or by any means, without the prior written permission of the copyright owner, except for the use of brief quotation in a book review.

To request permission, contact the publisher at info@whats4upublishing.com

ISBN: 978-1-7372717-0-3

Library of Congress Number: 2021915569

First paperback edition August 2021

Edited by: Jefferey Spivey

Cover art by: Ultrakhan22

Art by: Mya Booker and Machila Gates

Printed by What's 4U Publishing in the United States

What's 4U Publishing
PO Box 78593
Indianapolis, IN 46278

www.whats4Upublishing.com

ADULTING IS A TRIP

Navigating Through the Journey of Adulthood

**Ranada Dalton, LMHC, MAMFT, LPC
& Athena Salisbury**

What's 4 U Publishing

Thank you

First, we want to thank God for blessing us throughout the process of creating this workbook. Second, we want to thank any and everyone who had anything to do with the creation of our workbook. We would especially like to thank Machila and Mya for their amazing artwork contribution. Lastly, thank you to anyone who purchased (for themselves or others) or used this workbook. Adulthood can be challenging, but we must celebrate all wins!

Dedication

This journey called Life can be a challenge to navigate. As the saying goes, "life happens", regardless of whether we're ready for it or not. We would like to dedicate this book to the loved ones who inspired us to cultivate this workbook and navigate through life:

Nana, Granny, Aunt Sharan, Beverly, Makayla, Nedra, and the plethora of other influential people in our lives.

Confidence comes from creating something and knowing what I'm supposed to be doing and feeling like I'm good at what I'm supposed to be doing. -Issa Rae

WELCOME & CONGRATULATIONS

Empowered Living Inc. (ELI) wants to thank you for purchasing this workbook and starting the journey to a better you. We are uber-excited about all the goals you'll accomplish and the ways your life will transform by the end of the year.

"Winning in real life looks very different than it does on social media. Stay focused." - Jae Hardwick

CONTENTS

● FUTURE ME: LAYING THE FOUNDATION

Personal Vision & Mission Statement
Letter to Self
Encouragement Letters
No Regrets List
Prayer List
Goals
Goal Tracker
Yearly Goals
To Do Checklist
Task Tracker
Saving Tracker
Fitness Tracker
My Workout Challenge
Weight Loss Goals

● GET YOUR MIND RIGHT: MENTAL HEALTH

Forgiveness Letter
I'm feeling...Emotional Check-in
Mental Release
I'm Grateful For
Make Time for Self Care Suggestions
Make Time for Self Care Action Plan
Meditation Checklist
Gratitude
A Blessing in the Lessons

● ADULTING: GETTING YOUR AFFAIRS IN ORDER

Getting Your Affairs in Order Checklist
Emergency Binder

● BONUS POINTS

My Password Tracker
Birthday Reminders
Contacts
Travel Planning
Travel Itinerary
Coloring pages
Notes

Sometimes blessings come in the form of a hard time or a difficult situation.

DMX

GETTING STARTED
READ THIS FIRST

The purpose of this workbook is to provide some of the tools for this journey called life. The workbook is designed to be user-friendly and can be used at your own pace. One of the unique things about the workbook is that you don't have to use it in order for it to be useful, with the exception of Chapter 1.

It is recommended that you start with Chapter 1, *Future Me: Laying the Foundation*. The purpose of this section is to lay the foundation for the remainder of the workbook. In this chapter, we ask you to write a letter to your future self (e.g., you 365 days from the completion of the letter.).We also ask you to have others do the same thing on your behalf. As tempting as it may be, don't look at them.

Other things you'll do in this chapter include establishing goals, creating a "no regrets" list, action plans, and more. Once this chapter has been completed, feel free to move around the workbook. Worksheets are categorized by various topics, including mental health, finances, and getting your affairs in order. We recognize that not every subject or activity in the workbook will apply to you. This may be a season where it just isn't relevant and that's OK. Maybe it can apply to someone else; remember, sharing is caring!

The more frequently you use the workbook, the more useful it will be. We encourage you to use it at least once a week. Take your time as you complete the worksheets. It is not meant for you to rush. Instead, really take your time to provide thoughtful and meaningful answers. Keep in mind, you're doing this work for future you and for generations to come.

Adulting is a Trip: Navigating the Journey of Adulthood

Disclaimer

This workbook is designed to be a relevant guide that provides information and motivation to our readers. This workbook was sold with the understanding that the authors and publishing company are not engaging in rendering any type(s) of psychological, legal, financial, or other professional services by publishing this workbook. As each individual situation is unique, questions relevant to the reader's personal situation should be addressed by an appropriate professional. Doing so ensures that the specific situation has been evaluated professionally, carefully, and accurately in accordance to the individual. The authors and publisher are not liable for any psychological, emotional, financial, physical, or commercial damages. The authors' and publishing company's views are: You are responsible for your own actions, decisions, and consequences (whether positive or negative).

Visit our website at www.empoweredlivinginc.net
Send us an email to keep us updated on your progress.
info@empoweredlivinginc.net

Introduction:
The why behind this workbook

So…I bet you're wondering why we wrote this workbook and who we are. Well, the honest and short answer is that this workbook came out of necessity, but first, let us give you a little background. We are two-thirds of Empowered Living, a mental health practice in Indianapolis, IN. Our mission is to create a space for change by exercising awareness and accountability during the journey to healing.

Over the past few years, there have been several occasions where the idea of adulting has come up. Hence what lead us to think, "Maybe we should have a workshop about adulting?" We started by offering financial workshops across a variety of topics. From those workshops, we realized that there were several topics we weren't even touching. After brainstorming several ideas (multiple times),we decided to write a book. As we started the process of writing, we eventually decided the best route would be to create a workbook. We wanted to create something that was very interactive but could reach a broader spectrum of individuals.

From a personal standpoint, I think it's fair to say Athena and I have had several experiences that made the workbook an absolute necessity. Both of us have had our worlds turned upside down by life (on more than one occasion), including but not limited to death, divorce, financial scarcity, birth, and business. By going through these personal experiences (together in some cases), we learned a lot about what we didn't know. This led us to start the process of educating ourselves. This education came in the form of engaging with several experts, classes, workshops, books, and other resources; we wanted to be able to share our knowledge with others. Now, let's be clear, by no means are we saying we're experts in adulting, because that would be a lie. But we have been able to put together a starting point. The worksheets and resources we've assembled are things we tried ourselves or were strongly suggested by experts. The journey of adulthood is an interesting one, but our hope is that these tools will make it a little easier.

Let the journey begin! There will be mishaps but how you change the game will be your legacy.

With love,

Ranada & Athena

Future me: Laying the foundation

Stop letting people who do so little for you
control so much of your mind,
feelings, and emotions.

Will Smith

My Personal Vision/ Mission Statement

JUST LIKE IT'S IMPORTANT FOR A BUSINESS TO HAVE A VISION TO KNOW WHERE THEY ARE GOING AND A MISSION TO KNOW WHAT IT STANDS FOR, SO SHOULD YOU. CREATE A VISION AND MISSION STATEMENT THAT ARE SYMBOLIC OF HOW YOU LIVE YOUR LIFE OR PLAN TO LIVE IT IN THE FUTURE.

PERSONAL VISION STATMENT	MISSION STATEMENT

NOTES

You just have to start somewhere.- Anonymous

Letter to Self

Who doesn't like receiving positive mail?! Write a letter to the person you'll be in 365 days from now. In this letter, include goals, dreams, affirmations, desires, and well wishes. Once the letter has been completed, remove it from the workbook and place it in an envelope. On the 365th day, open it up and read what you wrote. *Add the date on your calendar so you won't forget.

_____

_____

_____

_____

_____

_____

_____

_____

_____

_____

_____

_____

_____

Encouragement Letters

Thank you for taking the time to write this letter. Words of affirmations are important. In this letter, offer up affirmations, wishes, prayers, and more to your loved one. Once the letter is complete, place it in an envelope and give it back sealed. On the 365th day, they will read your letter.

Encouragement Letters

Thank you for taking the time to write this letter. Words of affirmations are important. In this letter, offer up affirmations, wishes, prayers, and more to your loved one. Once the letter is complete, place it in an envelope and give it back sealed. On the 365th day, they will read your letter.

Encouragement Letters

Thank you for taking the time to write this letter. Words of affirmations are important. In this letter, offer up affirmations, wishes, prayers, and more to your loved one. Once the letter is complete, place it in an envelope and give it back sealed. On the 365th day, they will read your letter.

Encouragement Letters

Thank you for taking the time to write this letter. Words of affirmations are important. In this letter, offer up affirmations, wishes, prayers, and more to your loved one. Once the letter is complete, place it in an envelope and give it back sealed. On the 365th day, they will read your letter.

Encouragement Letters

Thank you for taking the time to write this letter. Words of affirmations are important. In this letter, offer up affirmations, wishes, prayers, and more to your loved one. Once the letter is complete, place it in an envelope and give it back sealed. On the 365th day, they will read your letter.

My No Regrets List

I WANT TO LIVE WITH NO REGRETS

The purpose of this activity is to create a list of experiences. The only rule is NOT TO PLACE LIMITS ON YOURSELF! Be as creative and ridiculous as possible. Some examples include traveling to each continent, establishing a scholarship, finishing your weekly to-do list, trying something new, learning a new skill or exploring a new subject, saving $3/$30/$300 a week/month, climbing a mountain, and/or running a marathon. You are only limited by the breadth of your imagination.

There are no new ideas. There are only new ways of making them felt. –Audre Lorde

My No Regrets List

Confidence comes from creating something and knowing what I'm supposed to be doing and feeling like I'm good at what I'm supposed to be doing. -Issa Rae

Prayer List

YOU HAVE NOT BECAUSE YOU DON'T ASK

Who or what are you praying for? Let out your desires and leave them here

How is the prayer manifesting? For example, if I'm praying for patience, I may notice increased opportunities for me to practice it.

Praise report(s) and lesson(s) learned even when things are not what I desire.

Prayer List

YOU HAVE NOT BECAUSE YOU DON'T ASK

Who or what are you praying for? Let out your desires and leave them here

How is the prayer manifesting? For example, if I'm praying for patience, I may notice increased opportunities for me to practice it.

Praise report(s) and lesson(s) learned even when things are not what I desire.

Prayer List

YOU HAVE NOT BECAUSE YOU DON'T ASK

Who or what are you praying for? Let out your desires and leave them here

How is the prayer manifesting? For example, if I'm praying for patience, I may notice increased opportunities for me to practice it.

Praise report(s) and lesson(s) learned even when things are not what I desire.

Prayer List

YOU HAVE NOT BECAUSE YOU DON'T ASK

Who or what are you praying for? Let out your desires and leave them here

How is the prayer manifesting? For example, if I'm praying for patience, I may notice increased opportunities for me to practice it.

Praise report(s) and lesson(s) learned even when things are not what I desire.

Prayer List

YOU HAVE NOT BECAUSE YOU DON'T ASK

Who or what are you praying for? Let out your desires and leave them here

How is the prayer manifesting? For example, if I'm praying for patience, I may notice increased opportunities for me to practice it.

Praise report(s) and lesson(s) learned even when things are not what I desire.

Prayer List

YOU HAVE NOT BECAUSE YOU DON'T ASK

Who or what are you praying for? Let out your desires and leave them here

How is the prayer manifesting? For example, if I'm praying for patience, I may notice increased opportunities for me to practice it.

Praise report(s) and lesson(s) learned even when things are not what I desire.

Prayer List

YOU HAVE NOT BECAUSE YOU DON'T ASK

Who or what are you praying for? Let out your desires and leave them here

How is the prayer manifesting? For example, if I'm praying for patience, I may notice increased opportunities for me to practice it.

Praise report(s) and lesson(s) learned even when things are not what I desire.

Prayer List

YOU HAVE NOT BECAUSE YOU DON'T ASK

Who or what are you praying for? Let out your desires and leave them here

How is the prayer manifesting? For example, if I'm praying for patience, I may notice increased opportunities for me to practice it.

Praise report(s) and lesson(s) learned even when things are not what I desire.

Prayer List

YOU HAVE NOT BECAUSE YOU DON'T ASK

Who or what are you praying for? Let out your desires and leave them here

How is the prayer manifesting? For example, if I'm praying for patience, I may notice increased opportunities for me to practice it.

Praise report(s) and lesson(s) learned even when things are not what I desire.

Prayer List

YOU HAVE NOT BECAUSE YOU DON'T ASK

Who or what are you praying for? Let out your desires and leave them here

How is the prayer manifesting? For example, if I'm praying for patience, I may notice increased opportunities for me to practice it.

Praise report(s) and lesson(s) learned even when things are not what I desire.

Prayer List

YOU HAVE NOT BECAUSE YOU DON'T ASK

Who or what are you praying for? Let out your desires and leave them here

How is the prayer manifesting? For example, if I'm praying for patience, I may notice increased opportunities for me to practice it.

Praise report(s) and lesson(s) learned even when things are not what I desire.

Prayer List

YOU HAVE NOT BECAUSE YOU DON'T ASK

Who or what are you praying for? Let out your desires and leave them here

How is the prayer manifesting? For example, if I'm praying for patience, I may notice increased opportunities for me to practice it.

Praise report(s) and lesson(s) learned even when things are not what I desire.

Goals

Goals are an important part of life. Use these next few pages to create goals and action plans. It's important to not just create the goals but have an action plan to help you move from thought to accomplishment. In this area, keep in mind the acronym M.O.V.E.:

M: Motivation. What is your why for this goal? It's not uncommon for us to want to accomplish something, but lack a strong enough why to keep us motivated. For example, let's say my goal is to save $1,000 within a year. I may not be as motivated to do it simply because it's a good idea. I would be more motivated if I reflected on my personal experience of not having savings, how that affected me, and my desire not to experience that again.

O: Observation. What is needed to accomplish this goal? During the observation period, use this time to do a brain dump. The benefit of a brain dump is it provides you an opportunity to get out of your head. While doing the dump, you should do two things. The first is to list everything that comes to mind for the topic, even if it doesn't make sense at the time. Next, create a list of what the potential barriers are. With these barriers, ask yourself how realistic it is for them to occur. What can be done to minimize the barriers?
Based on these lists, create your action plan. Remember that your actions don't have to be ridiculous. You can't build a house in a day; you can simply start with doing the research. Make sure that your plan is realistic for your expectations.

V: Validation. This step is where you put your plan to work. What is your timeline? Are your benchmarks realistic? Who are your accountability partners? Who are the people who hold you accountable and provide the necessary feedback?

E: Enjoy yourself. These are goals that you have created. It's easy to become so task-oriented. There is always a time and place for that, but you also want to enjoy the process. It's OK to take your time to learn from those experiences and see if those skills can be applied.

GOAL TRACKER

YOU SET THE GOAL AND GO!!

Weekly: _____   My Goal: _____

ACTION	TIME ALLOTTED

GOALS

- [ ] _____
- [ ] _____
- [ ] _____
- [ ] _____
- [ ] _____
- [ ] _____

NOTES

_____
_____
_____
_____
_____
_____

If I didn't define myself for myself, I would be crunched into other people's fantasies for me and eaten alive. —Audre Lorde

GOAL TRACKER

YOU SET THE GOAL AND GO!!

Weekly: ☐ My Goal: ☐

ACTION	TIME ALLOTTED

GOALS

☐ _____
☐ _____
☐ _____
☐ _____
☐ _____
☐ _____

NOTES

GOAL TRACKER

YOU SET THE GOAL AND GO!!

Weekly: _____ My Goal: _____

ACTION	TIME ALLOTTED

GOALS

- [ ] _____
- [ ] _____
- [ ] _____
- [ ] _____
- [ ] _____
- [ ] _____

NOTES

GOAL TRACKER

YOU SET THE GOAL AND GO!!

Weekly: _____   My Goal: _____

ACTION	TIME ALLOTTED

GOALS

- [ ] _____
- [ ] _____
- [ ] _____
- [ ] _____
- [ ] _____
- [ ] _____

NOTES

....
....
....
....
....
....

GOAL TRACKER

YOU SET THE GOAL AND GO!!

Weekly: _____   My Goal: _____

ACTION	TIME ALLOTTED

GOALS

- [ ] _____
- [ ] _____
- [ ] _____
- [ ] _____
- [ ] _____
- [ ] _____

NOTES

....
....
....
....
....
....
....

GOAL TRACKER

YOU SET THE GOAL AND GO!!

Weekly: _____   My Goal: _____

ACTION	TIME ALLOTTED

GOALS

- ☐ _____
- ☐ _____
- ☐ _____
- ☐ _____
- ☐ _____
- ☐ _____

NOTES

....

....

....

....

....

....

GOAL TRACKER

YOU SET THE GOAL AND GO!!

Weekly: _____   My Goal: _____

ACTION	TIME ALLOTTED

GOALS

- [ ] _____
- [ ] _____
- [ ] _____
- [ ] _____
- [ ] _____
- [ ] _____

NOTES

....
....
....
....
....
....

GOAL TRACKER

YOU SET THE GOAL AND GO!!

Weekly: _____   My Goal: _____

ACTION	TIME ALLOTTED

GOALS

- [ ] _____
- [ ] _____
- [ ] _____
- [ ] _____
- [ ] _____
- [ ] _____

NOTES

....
....
....
....
....
....
....

GOAL TRACKER

YOU SET THE GOAL AND GO!!

Weekly: _____   My Goal: _____

ACTION	TIME ALLOTTED

GOALS

- [ ] _____
- [ ] _____
- [ ] _____
- [ ] _____
- [ ] _____
- [ ] _____

NOTES

....
....
....
....
....
....
....

GOAL TRACKER

YOU SET THE GOAL AND GO!!

Weekly: _____   My Goal: _____

ACTION	TIME ALLOTTED

GOALS

- [ ] _____
- [ ] _____
- [ ] _____
- [ ] _____
- [ ] _____
- [ ] _____

NOTES

....
....
....
....
....
....
....

GOAL TRACKER

YOU SET THE GOAL AND GO!!

Weekly: _____   My Goal: _____

ACTION	TIME ALLOTTED

GOALS

- [ ] _____
- [ ] _____
- [ ] _____
- [ ] _____
- [ ] _____
- [ ] _____

NOTES

....
....
....
....
....
....
....

GOAL TRACKER

YOU SET THE GOAL AND GO!!

Weekly: _____ My Goal: _____

ACTION	TIME ALLOTTED

GOALS

- [ ] _____
- [ ] _____
- [ ] _____
- [ ] _____
- [ ] _____
- [ ] _____

NOTES

....
....
....
....
....
....

YEARLY GOALS

January	February	March
○ _____	○ _____	○ _____
○ _____	○ _____	○ _____
○ _____	○ _____	○ _____
○ _____	○ _____	○ _____

April	May	June
○ _____	○ _____	○ _____
○ _____	○ _____	○ _____
○ _____	○ _____	○ _____
○ _____	○ _____	○ _____

July	August	September
○ _____	○ _____	○ _____
○ _____	○ _____	○ _____
○ _____	○ _____	○ _____
○ _____	○ _____	○ _____

October	November	December
○ _____	○ _____	○ _____
○ _____	○ _____	○ _____
○ _____	○ _____	○ _____
○ _____	○ _____	○ _____

YEARLY GOALS
(For added goals)

January	February	March
○ _____	○ _____	○ _____
○ _____	○ _____	○ _____
○ _____	○ _____	○ _____
○ _____	○ _____	○ _____

April	May	June
○ _____	○ _____	○ _____
○ _____	○ _____	○ _____
○ _____	○ _____	○ _____
○ _____	○ _____	○ _____

July	August	September
○ _____	○ _____	○ _____
○ _____	○ _____	○ _____
○ _____	○ _____	○ _____
○ _____	○ _____	○ _____

October	November	December
○ _____	○ _____	○ _____
○ _____	○ _____	○ _____
○ _____	○ _____	○ _____
○ _____	○ _____	○ _____

TO DO CHECKLIST

NOTES

TO DO CHECKLIST

NOTES

TO DO CHECKLIST

NOTES

TO DO CHECKLIST

NOTES

TO DO CHECKLIST

NOTES

TO DO CHECKLIST

NOTES

TO DO CHECKLIST

NOTES

TO DO CHECKLIST

NOTES

TO DO CHECKLIST

NOTES

TO DO CHECKLIST

NOTES

TO DO CHECKLIST

NOTES

TO DO CHECKLIST

NOTES

TASK TRACKER

USE THIS PAGE TO STAY ON TASK

IMPORTANT TASKS

- [ ] _____
- [ ] _____
- [ ] _____
- [ ] _____
- [ ] _____
- [ ] _____
- [ ] _____
- [ ] _____
- [ ] _____

NEXT STEP

SKETCH IT OUT

TASK TRACKER

USE THIS PAGE TO STAY ON TASK

IMPORTANT TASKS

- [ ] _____
- [ ] _____
- [ ] _____
- [ ] _____
- [ ] _____
- [ ] _____
- [ ] _____
- [ ] _____
- [ ] _____

NEXT STEP

SKETCH IT OUT

TASK TRACKER

USE THIS PAGE TO STAY ON TASK

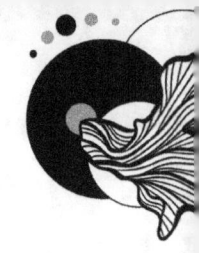

IMPORTANT TASKS

- [ ] _____
- [ ] _____
- [ ] _____
- [ ] _____
- [ ] _____
- [ ] _____
- [ ] _____
- [ ] _____
- [ ] _____

NEXT STEP

SKETCH IT OUT

TASK TRACKER

USE THIS PAGE TO STAY ON TASK

IMPORTANT TASKS ## NEXT STEP

- ☐ _____
- ☐ _____
- ☐ _____
- ☐ _____
- ☐ _____
- ☐ _____
- ☐ _____
- ☐ _____
- ☐ _____

SKETCH IT OUT

TASK TRACKER

USE THIS PAGE TO STAY ON TASK

IMPORTANT TASKS

- [ ] _____
- [ ] _____
- [ ] _____
- [ ] _____
- [ ] _____
- [ ] _____
- [ ] _____
- [ ] _____
- [ ] _____

NEXT STEP

SKETCH IT OUT

TASK TRACKER

USE THIS PAGE TO STAY ON TASK

IMPORTANT TASKS

NEXT STEP

- [ ] _____
- [ ] _____
- [ ] _____
- [ ] _____
- [ ] _____
- [ ] _____
- [ ] _____
- [ ] _____
- [ ] _____

SKETCH IT OUT

TASK TRACKER

USE THIS PAGE TO STAY ON TASK

IMPORTANT TASKS

- [ ] _____
- [ ] _____
- [ ] _____
- [ ] _____
- [ ] _____
- [ ] _____
- [ ] _____
- [ ] _____
- [ ] _____

NEXT STEP

SKETCH IT OUT

TASK TRACKER

USE THIS PAGE TO STAY ON TASK

IMPORTANT TASKS

NEXT STEP

- [ ] _____
- [ ] _____
- [ ] _____
- [ ] _____
- [ ] _____
- [ ] _____
- [ ] _____
- [ ] _____
- [ ] _____

SKETCH IT OUT

TASK TRACKER

USE THIS PAGE TO STAY ON TASK

IMPORTANT TASKS

- [ ] _____
- [ ] _____
- [ ] _____
- [ ] _____
- [ ] _____
- [ ] _____
- [ ] _____
- [ ] _____
- [ ] _____

NEXT STEP

SKETCH IT OUT

TASK TRACKER

USE THIS PAGE TO STAY ON TASK

IMPORTANT TASKS

- [ ] _____
- [ ] _____
- [ ] _____
- [ ] _____
- [ ] _____
- [ ] _____
- [ ] _____
- [ ] _____
- [ ] _____

NEXT STEP

SKETCH IT OUT

TASK TRACKER

USE THIS PAGE TO STAY ON TASK

IMPORTANT TASKS

- [ ] _____
- [ ] _____
- [ ] _____
- [ ] _____
- [ ] _____
- [ ] _____
- [ ] _____
- [ ] _____
- [ ] _____

NEXT STEP

SKETCH IT OUT

TASK TRACKER

USE THIS PAGE TO STAY ON TASK

IMPORTANT TASKS

- [ ] _____
- [ ] _____
- [ ] _____
- [ ] _____
- [ ] _____
- [ ] _____
- [ ] _____
- [ ] _____
- [ ] _____

NEXT STEP

SKETCH IT OUT

Anyone who has ever struggled with poverty knows how extremely expensive it is to be poor. - James Baldwin

Saving Tracker

GOAL:

SAVING:

DATE	AMOUNT

WEEK 1 TOTAL:

WEEK 2 TOTAL:

WEEK 3 TOTAL:

WEEK 4 TOTAL:

Saving Tracker

GOAL:

SAVING:

DATE	AMOUNT

WEEK 1 TOTAL:

WEEK 2 TOTAL:

WEEK 3 TOTAL:

WEEK 4 TOTAL:

Saving Tracker

GOAL:

SAVING:

DATE	AMOUNT

WEEK 1 TOTAL:

WEEK 2 TOTAL:

WEEK 3 TOTAL:

WEEK 4 TOTAL:

Saving Tracker

GOAL:

SAVING:

DATE	AMOUNT

WEEK 1 TOTAL:

WEEK 2 TOTAL:

WEEK 3 TOTAL:

WEEK 4 TOTAL:

Saving Tracker

GOAL:

SAVING:

DATE	AMOUNT

WEEK 1 TOTAL:

WEEK 2 TOTAL:

WEEK 3 TOTAL:

WEEK 4 TOTAL:

Saving Tracker

GOAL:

SAVING:

DATE	AMOUNT

WEEK 1 TOTAL:

WEEK 2 TOTAL:

WEEK 3 TOTAL:

WEEK 4 TOTAL:

Saving Tracker

GOAL:

SAVING:

DATE	AMOUNT

WEEK 1 TOTAL:

WEEK 2 TOTAL:

WEEK 3 TOTAL:

WEEK 4 TOTAL:

Saving Tracker

GOAL:

SAVING:

DATE	AMOUNT

WEEK 1 TOTAL:

WEEK 2 TOTAL:

WEEK 3 TOTAL:

WEEK 4 TOTAL:

Saving Tracker

GOAL:

SAVING:

DATE	AMOUNT

WEEK 1 TOTAL:

WEEK 2 TOTAL:

WEEK 3 TOTAL:

WEEK 4 TOTAL:

Saving Tracker

GOAL:

SAVING:

DATE	AMOUNT

WEEK 1 TOTAL:

WEEK 2 TOTAL:

WEEK 3 TOTAL:

WEEK 4 TOTAL:

Saving Tracker

GOAL:

SAVING:

DATE	AMOUNT

WEEK 1 TOTAL:

WEEK 2 TOTAL:

WEEK 3 TOTAL:

WEEK 4 TOTAL:

Saving Tracker

GOAL:

SAVING:

DATE	AMOUNT

WEEK 1 TOTAL:

WEEK 2 TOTAL:

WEEK 3 TOTAL:

WEEK 4 TOTAL:

FITNESS TRACKER

YOU SET THE GOAL AND GO!!

Weekly: ☐   My Goal: ☐

ACTIVITY	TIME / DISTANCE

WATER GOAL

☐ 🥛🥛🥛🥛🥛🥛🥛🥛
☐ 🥛🥛🥛🥛🥛🥛🥛🥛
☐ 🥛🥛🥛🥛🥛🥛🥛🥛
☐ 🥛🥛🥛🥛🥛🥛🥛🥛
☐ 🥛🥛🥛🥛🥛🥛🥛🥛
☐ 🥛🥛🥛🥛🥛🥛🥛🥛
☐ 🥛🥛🥛🥛🥛🥛🥛🥛

GOALS

☐ _____
☐ _____
☐ _____
☐ _____

NOTES

....
....
....
....
....

FITNESS TRACKER

YOU SET THE GOAL AND GO!!

Weekly: ☐   My Goal: ☐

ACTIVITY	TIME / DISTANCE

WATER GOAL

☐
☐
☐
☐
☐
☐
☐

GOALS

☐ _____
☐ _____
☐ _____
☐ _____

NOTES

....
....
....
....

FITNESS TRACKER

YOU SET THE GOAL AND GO!!

Weekly: _____   My Goal: _____

ACTIVITY	TIME / DISTANCE

WATER GOAL

☐ 🥛🥛🥛🥛🥛🥛🥛
☐ 🥛🥛🥛🥛🥛🥛🥛
☐ 🥛🥛🥛🥛🥛🥛🥛
☐ 🥛🥛🥛🥛🥛🥛🥛
☐ 🥛🥛🥛🥛🥛🥛🥛
☐ 🥛🥛🥛🥛🥛🥛🥛
☐ 🥛🥛🥛🥛🥛🥛🥛

GOALS

☐ _____
☐ _____
☐ _____
☐ _____

NOTES

....
....
....
....
....

FITNESS TRACKER

YOU SET THE GOAL AND GO!!

Weekly: _____   My Goal: _____

ACTIVITY	TIME / DISTANCE

WATER GOAL

☐ ☐ ☐ ☐ ☐ ☐ ☐

GOALS

☐ _____
☐ _____
☐ _____
☐ _____

NOTES

....
....
....
....
....

FITNESS TRACKER

YOU SET THE GOAL AND GO!!

Weekly: ☐   My Goal: ☐

ACTIVITY	TIME / DISTANCE

WATER GOAL

☐ 🥛🥛🥛🥛🥛🥛🥛🥛
☐ 🥛🥛🥛🥛🥛🥛🥛🥛
☐ 🥛🥛🥛🥛🥛🥛🥛🥛
☐ 🥛🥛🥛🥛🥛🥛🥛🥛
☐ 🥛🥛🥛🥛🥛🥛🥛🥛
☐ 🥛🥛🥛🥛🥛🥛🥛🥛
☐ 🥛🥛🥛🥛🥛🥛🥛🥛

GOALS

☐ _____
☐ _____
☐ _____
☐ _____

NOTES

....
....
....
....
....

FITNESS TRACKER

YOU SET THE GOAL AND GO!!

Weekly: _____   My Goal: _____

ACTIVITY	TIME / DISTANCE

WATER GOAL

☐ 🥛🥛🥛🥛🥛🥛🥛🥛
☐ 🥛🥛🥛🥛🥛🥛🥛🥛
☐ 🥛🥛🥛🥛🥛🥛🥛🥛
☐ 🥛🥛🥛🥛🥛🥛🥛🥛
☐ 🥛🥛🥛🥛🥛🥛🥛🥛
☐ 🥛🥛🥛🥛🥛🥛🥛🥛
☐ 🥛🥛🥛🥛🥛🥛🥛🥛

GOALS

☐ _____
☐ _____
☐ _____
☐ _____

NOTES

....
....
....
....
....

FITNESS TRACKER

YOU SET THE GOAL AND GO!!

Weekly: _____   My Goal: _____

ACTIVITY	TIME / DISTANCE

WATER GOAL

☐ 🥛🥛🥛🥛🥛🥛🥛🥛
☐ 🥛🥛🥛🥛🥛🥛🥛🥛
☐ 🥛🥛🥛🥛🥛🥛🥛🥛
☐ 🥛🥛🥛🥛🥛🥛🥛🥛
☐ 🥛🥛🥛🥛🥛🥛🥛🥛
☐ 🥛🥛🥛🥛🥛🥛🥛🥛
☐ 🥛🥛🥛🥛🥛🥛🥛🥛

GOALS

☐ _____
☐ _____
☐ _____
☐ _____

NOTES

....
....
....
....
....

FITNESS TRACKER

YOU SET THE GOAL AND GO!!

Weekly: _____   My Goal: _____

ACTIVITY	TIME / DISTANCE

WATER GOAL

☐ 🥛🥛🥛🥛🥛🥛🥛🥛
☐ 🥛🥛🥛🥛🥛🥛🥛🥛
☐ 🥛🥛🥛🥛🥛🥛🥛🥛
☐ 🥛🥛🥛🥛🥛🥛🥛🥛
☐ 🥛🥛🥛🥛🥛🥛🥛🥛
☐ 🥛🥛🥛🥛🥛🥛🥛🥛
☐ 🥛🥛🥛🥛🥛🥛🥛🥛

GOALS

☐ _____
☐ _____
☐ _____
☐ _____

NOTES

....
....
....
....
....

FITNESS TRACKER

YOU SET THE GOAL AND GO!!

Weekly: _____   My Goal: _____

ACTIVITY	TIME / DISTANCE

WATER GOAL

☐ 🥛🥛🥛🥛🥛🥛🥛🥛
☐ 🥛🥛🥛🥛🥛🥛🥛🥛
☐ 🥛🥛🥛🥛🥛🥛🥛🥛
☐ 🥛🥛🥛🥛🥛🥛🥛🥛
☐ 🥛🥛🥛🥛🥛🥛🥛🥛
☐ 🥛🥛🥛🥛🥛🥛🥛🥛
☐ 🥛🥛🥛🥛🥛🥛🥛🥛

GOALS

☐ _____
☐ _____
☐ _____
☐ _____

NOTES

....
....
....
....
....

FITNESS TRACKER

YOU SET THE GOAL AND GO!!

Weekly: _____   My Goal: _____

ACTIVITY	TIME / DISTANCE

WATER GOAL

☐ 🥛🥛🥛🥛🥛🥛🥛🥛
☐ 🥛🥛🥛🥛🥛🥛🥛🥛
☐ 🥛🥛🥛🥛🥛🥛🥛🥛
☐ 🥛🥛🥛🥛🥛🥛🥛🥛
☐ 🥛🥛🥛🥛🥛🥛🥛🥛
☐ 🥛🥛🥛🥛🥛🥛🥛🥛
☐ 🥛🥛🥛🥛🥛🥛🥛🥛

GOALS

☐ _____
☐ _____
☐ _____
☐ _____

NOTES

....
....
....
....
....

FITNESS TRACKER

YOU SET THE GOAL AND GO!!

Weekly: _____   My Goal: _____

ACTIVITY	TIME / DISTANCE

WATER GOAL

☐ 🥛🥛🥛🥛🥛🥛🥛🥛
☐ 🥛🥛🥛🥛🥛🥛🥛🥛
☐ 🥛🥛🥛🥛🥛🥛🥛🥛
☐ 🥛🥛🥛🥛🥛🥛🥛🥛
☐ 🥛🥛🥛🥛🥛🥛🥛🥛
☐ 🥛🥛🥛🥛🥛🥛🥛🥛
☐ 🥛🥛🥛🥛🥛🥛🥛🥛

GOALS

☐ _____
☐ _____
☐ _____
☐ _____

NOTES

....
....
....
....
....

FITNESS TRACKER

YOU SET THE GOAL AND GO!!

Weekly: _____   My Goal: _____

ACTIVITY	TIME / DISTANCE

WATER GOAL

☐ 🥛🥛🥛🥛🥛🥛🥛🥛
☐ 🥛🥛🥛🥛🥛🥛🥛🥛
☐ 🥛🥛🥛🥛🥛🥛🥛🥛
☐ 🥛🥛🥛🥛🥛🥛🥛🥛
☐ 🥛🥛🥛🥛🥛🥛🥛🥛
☐ 🥛🥛🥛🥛🥛🥛🥛🥛
☐ 🥛🥛🥛🥛🥛🥛🥛🥛

GOALS

☐ _____
☐ _____
☐ _____
☐ _____

NOTES

....
....
....
....
....

MY WORKOUT CHALLENGE

DESIGN YOUR OWN WORKOUT CHALLENGE

☐

☐

☐

☐

☐

☐

"Sometimes you need to get knocked down before you can really figure out what your fight is and how you need to fight it." -Chadwick Bosemen

MY WORKOUT CHALLENGE

DESIGN YOUR OWN WORKOUT CHALLENGE

- [ ]
- [ ]
- [ ]
- [ ]
- [ ]
- [ ]

MY WORKOUT CHALLENGE

DESIGN YOUR OWN WORKOUT CHALLENGE

- [ ]
- [ ]
- [ ]
- [ ]
- [ ]
- [ ]

MY WORKOUT CHALLENGE

MY WORKOUT CHALLENGE

DESIGN YOUR OWN WORKOUT CHALLENGE

- [ ]
- [ ]
- [ ]
- [ ]
- [ ]
- [ ]

MY WORKOUT CHALLENGE

DESIGN YOUR OWN WORKOUT CHALLENGE

- [ ]
- [ ]
- [ ]
- [ ]
- [ ]
- [ ]

MY WORKOUT CHALLENGE

DESIGN YOUR OWN WORKOUT CHALLENGE

- [ ]
- [ ]
- [ ]
- [ ]
- [ ]
- [ ]

MY WORKOUT CHALLENGE

DESIGN YOUR OWN WORKOUT CHALLENGE

- [ ]
- [ ]
- [ ]
- [ ]
- [ ]
- [ ]

MY WORKOUT CHALLENGE

MY WORKOUT CHALLENGE

DESIGN YOUR OWN WORKOUT CHALLENGE

- [ ]
- [ ]
- [ ]
- [ ]
- [ ]
- [ ]

MY WORKOUT CHALLENGE

DESIGN YOUR OWN WORKOUT CHALLENGE

- [ ]
- [ ]
- [ ]
- [ ]
- [ ]
- [ ]

MY WORKOUT CHALLENGE

DESIGN YOUR OWN WORKOUT CHALLENGE

- [ ]
- [ ]
- [ ]
- [ ]
- [ ]
- [ ]

MY WORKOUT CHALLENGE

DESIGN YOUR OWN WORKOUT CHALLENGE

- [ ]
- [ ]
- [ ]
- [ ]
- [ ]
- [ ]

MY WORKOUT CHALLENGE

DESIGN YOUR OWN WORKOUT CHALLENGE

- [ ]
- [ ]
- [ ]
- [ ]
- [ ]
- [ ]

Weight Loss GOALS

Track Your Progress

Starting point

YOU GOT THIS!!

YOU DID IT!!

Be bold, be brave enough to be your true self. -Queen Latifah

Weight Loss GOALS

Track Your Progress

Starting point

YOU GOT THIS!!

YOU DID IT!!

Weight Loss GOALS

Track Your Progress

Starting poi[nt]

YOU GOT THIS!!

YOU DID IT!!

Weight Loss
GOALS

Track
Your Progress

Starting point

YOU GOT THIS!!

YOU DID IT!!

get your mind right: mental health

I don't know everything. I know a fraction of what there is to know, and I don't think I will ever know everything, but it's important to me to constantly challenge myself.

Yara Shahidi

Forgiveness Letter

According to the Oxford Dictionary, forgiveness is when you "stop feeling angry or resentful toward (someone) for an offense, flaw, or mistake" or "Cancel (a debt)". Forgiveness is more for you than the other person. Write a letter to someone(s) you need to forgive, yourself included, if needed.

Forgiveness isn't approving what happened. It's choosing to rise above it. -Robin Sharma

Forgiveness Letter

According to the Oxford Dictionary, forgiveness is when you "stop feeling angry or resentful toward (someone) for an offense, flaw, or mistake" or "Cancel (a debt)". Forgiveness is more for you than the other person. Write a letter to someone(s) you need to forgive, yourself included, if needed.

Forgiveness Letter

According to the Oxford Dictionary, forgiveness is when you "stop feeling angry or resentful toward (someone) for an offense, flaw, or mistake" or "Cancel (a debt)". Forgiveness is more for you than the other person. Write a letter to someone(s) you need to forgive, yourself included, if needed.

Forgiveness Letter

According to the Oxford Dictionary, forgiveness is when you "stop feeling angry or resentful toward (someone) for an offense, flaw, or mistake" or "Cancel (a debt)". Forgiveness is more for you than the other person. Write a letter to someone(s) you need to forgive, yourself included, if needed.

MENTAL RELEASE

What went well today?

Were there any challenges?

HOW ARE YOU EMOTIONALLY

The most common way people give up their power is by thinking they don't have any. –Alice Walker

MENTAL RELEASE

What went well today?

Were there any challenges?

HOW ARE YOU EMOTIONALLY

....

....

....

....

....

MENTAL RELEASE

What went well today?

Were there any challenges?

HOW ARE YOU EMOTIONALLY

MENTAL RELEASE

What went well today?

Were there any challenges?

HOW ARE YOU EMOTIONALLY

....
....
....
....
....

MENTAL RELEASE

What went well today?

Were there any challenges?

HOW ARE YOU EMOTIONALLY

MENTAL RELEASE

What went well today?

Were there any challenges?

HOW ARE YOU EMOTIONALLY

MENTAL RELEASE

What went well today?

Were there any challenges?

HOW ARE YOU EMOTIONALLY

MENTAL RELEASE

What went well today?

Were there any challenges?

HOW ARE YOU EMOTIONALLY

MENTAL RELEASE

What went well today?

Were there any challenges?

HOW ARE YOU EMOTIONALLY

MENTAL RELEASE

What went well today?

Were there any challenges?

HOW ARE YOU EMOTIONALLY

MENTAL RELEASE

What went well today?

Were there any challenges?

HOW ARE YOU EMOTIONALLY

MENTAL RELEASE

What went well today?

Were there any challenges?

HOW ARE YOU EMOTIONALLY

....
....
....
....
....

I'M FEELING...
EMOTIONAL CHECK-IN

Use this page to track your emotions and as an opportunity to journal more about your feelings. Try to be as open and vulnerable with yourself as possible.

Caring for myself is not self-indulgence, it is self-preservation, and that is an act of political warfare. —Audre Lorde

I'M FEELING...
EMOTIONAL CHECK-IN

Use this page to track your emotions and as an opportunity to journal more about your feelings. Try to be as open and vulnerable with yourself as possible.

I'M FEELING...
EMOTIONAL CHECK-IN

Use this page to track your emotions and as an opportunity to journal more about your feelings. Try to be as open and vulnerable with yourself as possible.

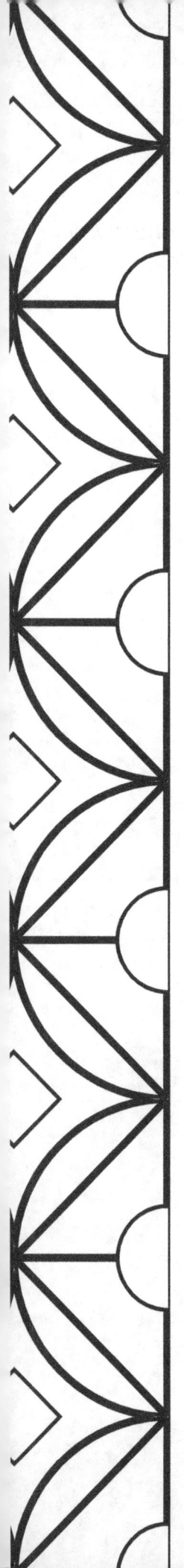

I'M FEELING...
EMOTIONAL CHECK-IN

Use this page to track your emotions and as an opportunity to journal more about you feelings. Try to be as open and vulnerable with yourself as possible.

I'M FEELING...

EMOTIONAL CHECK-IN

Use this page to track your emotions and as an opportunity to journal more about your feelings. Try to be as open and vulnerable with yourself as possible.

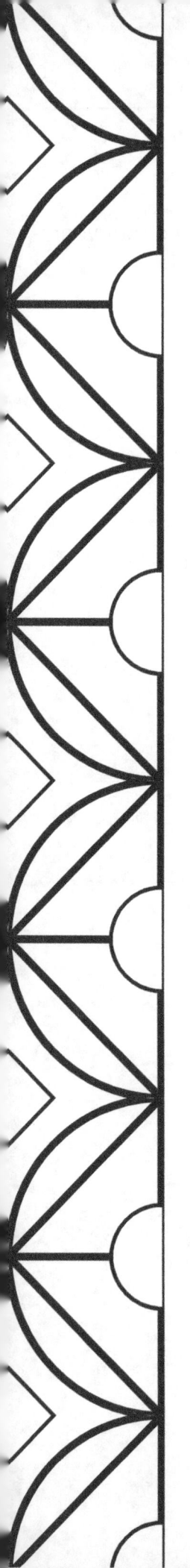

I'M FEELING...

EMOTIONAL CHECK-IN

Use this page to track your emotions and as an opportunity to journal more about your feelings. Try to be as open and vulnerable with yourself as possible.

I'M FEELING...

EMOTIONAL CHECK-IN

Use this page to track your emotions and as an opportunity to journal more about your feelings. Try to be as open and vulnerable with yourself as possible.

I'M FEELING...

EMOTIONAL CHECK-IN

Use this page to track your emotions and as an opportunity to journal more about you feelings. Try to be as open and vulnerable with yourself as possible.

_____
_____
_____
_____
_____
_____
_____
_____
_____
_____
_____
_____
_____
_____
_____
_____
_____
_____
_____
_____
_____
_____

I'M FEELING...

EMOTIONAL CHECK-IN

Use this page to track your emotions and as an opportunity to journal more about your feelings. Try to be as open and vulnerable with yourself as possible.

I'M FEELING...
EMOTIONAL CHECK-IN

Use this page to track your emotions and as an opportunity to journal more about your feelings. Try to be as open and vulnerable with yourself as possible.

I'M FEELING...

EMOTIONAL CHECK-IN

Use this page to track your emotions and as an opportunity to journal more about your feelings. Try to be as open and vulnerable with yourself as possible.

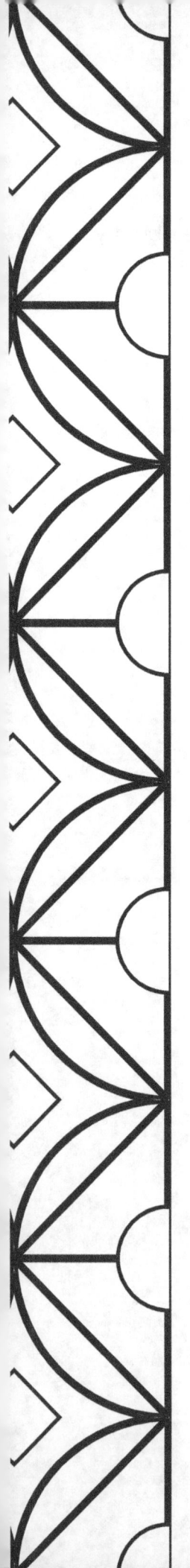

I'M FEELING...

EMOTIONAL CHECK-IN

Use this page to track your emotions and as an opportunity to journal more about you feelings. Try to be as open and vulnerable with yourself as possible.

I'm Grateful For
Thinking about Being Thankful

It's easy to sometimes forget the things we are grateful for. Use this space to reflect on what you're grateful for. Try to do this often and revisit the list when necessary.

Just because you have a nightmare doesn't mean you stop dreaming. -Jill Scott

You're worth more than platinum

I'm Grateful For

Thinking about Being Thankful

It's easy to sometimes forget the things we are grateful for. Use this space to reflect on what you're grateful for. Try to do this often and revisit the list when necessary.

_____
_____
_____
_____
_____
_____
_____
_____
_____
_____
_____
_____
_____

I'm Grateful For

Thinking about Being Thankful

It's easy to sometimes forget the things we are grateful for. Use this space to reflect on what you're grateful for. Try to do this often and revisit the list when necessary.

I'm Grateful For

Thinking about Being Thankful

It's easy to sometimes forget the things we are grateful for. Use this space to reflect on what you're grateful for. Try to do this often and revisit the list when necessary.

Gratitude

Create a list of things you are thankful for.

-We may encounter many defeats but we must not be defeated. -Maya Angelou

Gratitude

Create a list of things you are thankful for.

Gratitude

Create a list of things you are thankful for.

Gratitude

Create a list of things you are thankful for.

Gratitude

Create a list of things you are thankful for.

Gratitude

Create a list of things you are thankful for.

MAKE TIME FOR

Self-Care

Suggestions

- Track your mood
- Get more rest
- Time with family/Friends
- Meal with a friend
- Break from work
- Social media break
- Read
- Exercise
- Stay hydrated

- Gratitude list
- Get a massage
- Meal by myself
- Meditate
- Deep breathing
- Enjoy nature
- Sit in silence
- Journaling
- Eat healthy

Now it's your turn. Create an action plan

If you don't like something, change it. If you can't change it, change your attitude. -Mya Angelou

BRAINSTORM
Use this page to brainstorm your ideas!

MAKE TIME FOR
Self-Care

Action Plan
Create a plan to make yourself a priority. Review/update your plan at least once a quarter.

_____

_____

_____

_____

_____

_____

_____

_____

_____

You pray for rain, you gotta deal with the mud too. That's a part of it. -Denzel Washington

MAKE TIME FOR Self-Care

Action Plan
Create a plan to make yourself a priority. Review/update your plan at least once a quarter.

_____

_____

_____

_____

_____

_____

_____

_____

_____

_____

MAKE TIME FOR
Self-Care

Action Plan

Create a plan to make yourself a priority. Review/update your plan at least once a quarter.

_____

_____

_____

_____

_____

_____

_____

_____

_____

_____

MAKE TIME FOR

Action Plan
Create a plan to make yourself a priority. Review/update your plan at least once a quarter.

_____

_____

_____

_____

_____

_____

_____

_____

_____

Meditation Checklist

LET'S GET STARTED

- [ ] Take a moment to clear your mind.

- [ ] Turn your cell phone off/Do Not Disturb.

- [ ] Breathe in through your nose, hold for 10 seconds.

- [ ] Exhale through your mouth, emptying your lungs completely.
    (Repeat 3-5 times)

- [ ] Explore stretches you can incorporate.
    (Perform to your comfort level)

- [ ] Drink water.

- [ ] Allow yourself grace to have imperfect moments.

Start the day Happy and Relaxed- Set the Tone

YOU'RE ENOUGH BECAUSE YOU'VE ALWAYS BEEN

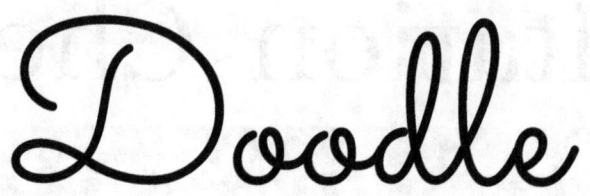

Use this space for whatever comes to mind

A BLESSING IN THE LESSONS

It's not always a curse, it can be a blessing

Use these pages to track your blessings/gratitude throughout the year.

_____
_____
_____
_____
_____
_____
_____
_____
_____
_____
_____
_____
_____
_____
_____
_____
_____

"The only difference between a hero and the villain is that the villain chooses to use that power in a way that is selfish and hurts other people." -Chadwick Boseman

A BLESSING IN THE LESSONS

It's not always a curse, it can be a blessing

Use these pages to track your blessings/gratitude throughout the year.

A BLESSING IN THE LESSONS

It's not always a curse, it can be a blessing

Use these pages to track your blessings/gratitude throughout the year.

A BLESSING IN THE LESSONS

It's not always a curse, it can be a blessing

Use these pages to track your blessings/gratitude throughout the year.

Adulting: getting your affairs in order

Whenever you are creating beauty around you, you are restoring your own soul.

Alice Walker

GETTING YOUR AFFAIRS IN ORDER

checklist

Cross off each item you complete or update this year.

- [ ] Annual health exam, specialist (if needed)

- [ ] Dental exam (twice a year) & Eye exam

- [ ] Update résumé/Curriculum Vitae (CV)

- [ ] Sign up for classes/courses

- [ ] Will and/or Trust (create or update)

- [ ] Insurance (life, home, renters, auto, etc.) – do you have enough?

- [ ] Budget (list of your debts, payments, income, etc.)

- [ ] License/ID (do you have any to renew or obtain?)

- [ ] FAFSA

- [ ] Memberships/Registrations (Do you actually use them all or are you donating?)

- [ ] Maintenance (auto and home)

- [ ] Check smoke detectors

- [ ] Check retirement documents (IRA, 401k, 403b, Pension, SEP) to maximize contributions.

- [ ] Use your HSA

- [ ] Create a home inventory, take photos, and put things on your insurance policy (including pets)

Love is forever but time is not. —Sharon D. Jones

Build your own checklist

Use this page to add any additional items

Emergency Binder

Make sure you have all of your important documents in one place in case of an emergency. These can be copies of the originals. Make sure you keep it in a safe place. Inform a trusted person about the binder, in case they need to access it on your behalf.

FAMILY/HOUSEHOLD

- [ ] Birth/Death/Marriage certificate
- [ ] Divorce decree/ adoption papers
- [ ] Social Security cards/Citizenship papers/ Passport
- [ ] Copies of driver's license (Have one on your phone also)
- [ ] Emergency contacts
- [ ] Family history/Photos (At least 1 up todate one)
- [ ] Passports
- [ ] License/Certifications/Trainings
- [ ] Insurance policies
- [ ] Household inventory/Photos/Receipts/ Warranties/Extra keys
- [ ] Transcripts/degrees/Diplomas
- [ ] Deeds/Titles
- [ ] Pet information
- [ ] Medical history/Immunizations/ Organ donor/Insurance cards/ Prescription list

END OF LIFE

- [ ] Wills/Living Wills/ Trust/Advance Directive/Power of Attonery
- [ ] Have list of passwords to access
- [ ] Letter of instructions/wishes
- [ ] Proof of ownership (Home, Auto, etc)

FINANCES

- [ ] Bank account inforrmation
- [ ] Stocks and bonds information
- [ ] Retirement information
- [ ] Taxes
- [ ] HSA/FSA information
- [ ] Government benefits information (Alimony, child support, SSI, etc)

Emergency Binder
Use this page to add any additional items

☐	☐
☐	☐
☐	☐
☐	☐
☐	☐
☐	☐
☐	☐

NOTES

Bonus Points

No person is your friend who demands your silence or denies your right to grow.

-Alice Walker

My Password Tracker

Password

Website:

User name:

Password:

Email:

Password

Website:

User name:

Password:

Email:

Password

Website:

User name:

Password:

Email:

Password

Website:

User name:

Password:

Email:

OTHER IMPORTANT INFORMATION

My Password Tracker

Password

Website:

User name:

Password:

Email:

Password

Website:

User name:

Password:

Email:

Password

Website:

User name:

Password:

Email:

Password

Website:

User name:

Password:

Email:

OTHER IMPORTANT INFORMATION

My Password Tracker

Password

Website:

User name:

Password:

Email:

Password

Website:

User name:

Password:

Email:

Password

Website:

User name:

Password:

Email:

Password

Website:

User name:

Password:

Email:

OTHER IMPORTANT INFORMATION

My Password Tracker

Password

Website:

User name:

Password:

Email:

Password

Website:

User name:

Password:

Email:

Password

Website:

User name:

Password:

Email:

Password

Website:

User name:

Password:

Email:

OTHER IMPORTANT INFORMATION

Birthday Reminder

January

February

March

April

May

June

July

August

September

October

November

December

Don't compare yourself to others. That's when you start to lose confidence in yourself.
Will Smith

Birthday Reminder

January

February

March

April

May

June

July

August

September

October

November

December

CONTACTS

Name:

Birthday:

Address:

Contact Number/s:

Email:

Name:

Birthday:

Home Address:

Contact Number/s:

Email:

Name:

Birthday:

Home Address:

Contact Number/s:

Email:

Name:

Birthday:

Home Address:

Contact Number/s:

Email:

Kindness costs nothing

CONTACTS

Name: _____ Birthday: _____

Address: _____

Contact Number/s: _____ Email: _____

_____

Name: _____ Birthday: _____

Home Address: _____

Contact Number/s: _____ Email: _____

_____

Name: _____ Birthday: _____

Home Address: _____

Contact Number/s: _____ Email: _____

_____

Name: _____ Birthday: _____

Home Address: _____

Contact Number/s: _____ Email: _____

_____

CONTACTS

Name: _____ Birthday: _____

Address: _____

Contact Number/s: _____ Email: _____

_____ _____

Name: _____ Birthday: _____

Home Address: _____

Contact Number/s: _____ Email: _____

_____ _____

Name: _____ Birthday: _____

Home Address: _____

Contact Number/s: _____ Email: _____

_____ _____

Name: _____ Birthday: _____

Home Address: _____

Contact Number/s: _____ Email: _____

_____ _____

CONTACTS

Name: _____ Birthday: _____

Address: _____

Contact Number/s: _____ Email: _____

_____ _____

Name: _____ Birthday: _____

Home Address: _____

Contact Number/s: _____ Email: _____

_____ _____

Name: _____ Birthday: _____

Home Address: _____

Contact Number/s: _____ Email: _____

_____ _____

Name: _____ Birthday: _____

Home Address: _____

Contact Number/s: _____ Email: _____

_____ _____

travel planning

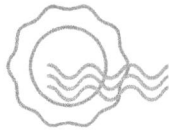

Destination

Dates

Adventures (Experiences & taste)

Adventures (What will you See & Visit)

ACTIVITY	COST		ACTIVITY	COST

"Humor is laughing at what you haven't got when you ought to have it." — Langston Hughes

travel itinerary

DESTINATION IDEAS:

DURATION OF STAY:

TIMEFRAME:

HOTEL DETAILS:

ARRIVAL:

DAY 1 — WHAT TO DO: — BUDGET:

DAY 2 — WHAT TO DO: — BUDGET:

DAY 3 — WHAT TO DO: — BUDGET:

DAY 4 — WHAT TO DO: — BUDGET:

travel planning

Destination

Dates

Adventures (Experiences & taste)

Adventures (What will you See & Visit)

ACTIVITY	COST

ACTIVITY	COST

travel itinerary

DESTINATION IDEAS:

DURATION OF STAY:

TIMEFRAME:

HOTEL DETAILS:

ARRIVAL:

DAY 1 — WHAT TO DO: — BUDGET:

DAY 2 — WHAT TO DO: — BUDGET:

DAY 3 — WHAT TO DO: — BUDGET:

DAY 4 — WHAT TO DO: — BUDGET:

travel planning

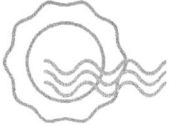

Destination

Dates

Adventures (Experiences & taste)

Adventures (What will you See & Visit)

ACTIVITY	COST		ACTIVITY	COST

travel itinerary

DESTINATION IDEAS:

DURATION OF STAY:

TIMEFRAME:

HOTEL DETAILS:

ARRIVAL:

DAY 1 — **WHAT TO DO:** — **BUDGET:**

DAY 2 — **WHAT TO DO:** — **BUDGET:**

DAY 3 — **WHAT TO DO:** — **BUDGET:**

DAY 4 — **WHAT TO DO:** — **BUDGET:**

travel planning

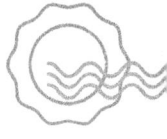

Destination

Dates

Adventures (Experiences & taste)

Adventures (What will you See & Visit)

ACTIVITY	COST

ACTIVITY	COST

travel itinerary

DESTINATION IDEAS:

DURATION OF STAY:

TIMEFRAME:

HOTEL DETAILS:

ARRIVAL:

DAY 1 — WHAT TO DO: — BUDGET:

DAY 2 — WHAT TO DO: — BUDGET:

DAY 3 — WHAT TO DO: — BUDGET:

DAY 4 — WHAT TO DO: — BUDGET:

travel planning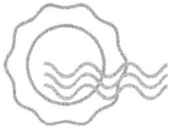

Destination

Dates

Adventures (Experiences & taste)

Adventures (What will you See & Visit)

ACTIVITY	COST

ACTIVITY	COST

Use the next few pages to color, doodle, take notes, etc.

Artwork created by Machila and Mya. Both ladies are high school students with amazing talent. If you are interested in their artwork, please contact them directly.

Machila Gates via email: bluchis4l@gmail.com
Mya Booker via Facebook: @myabooker

When someone shows you who they are, believe them the first time -Maya Angelou

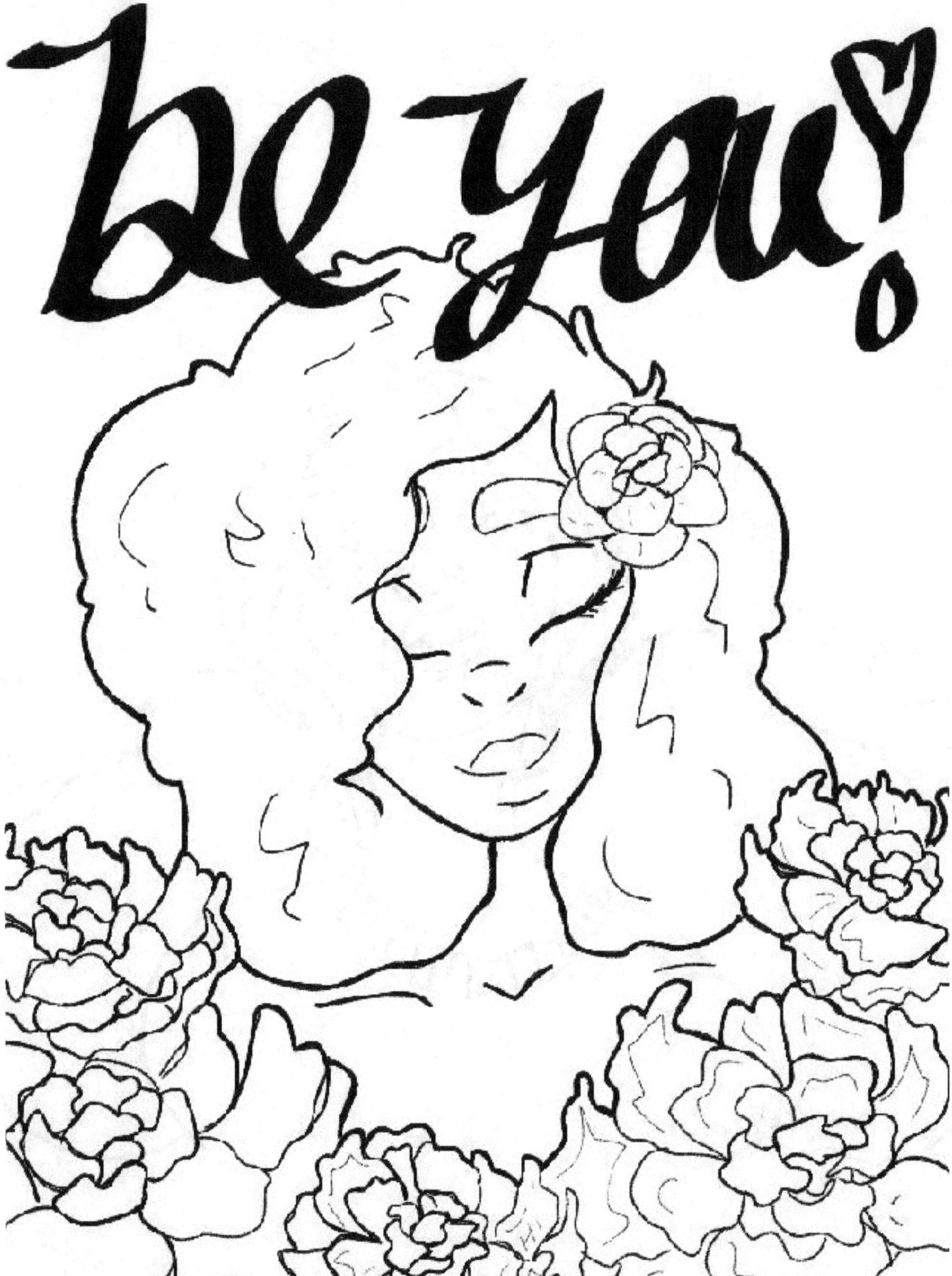
be you!

EMPOWERED LIVING

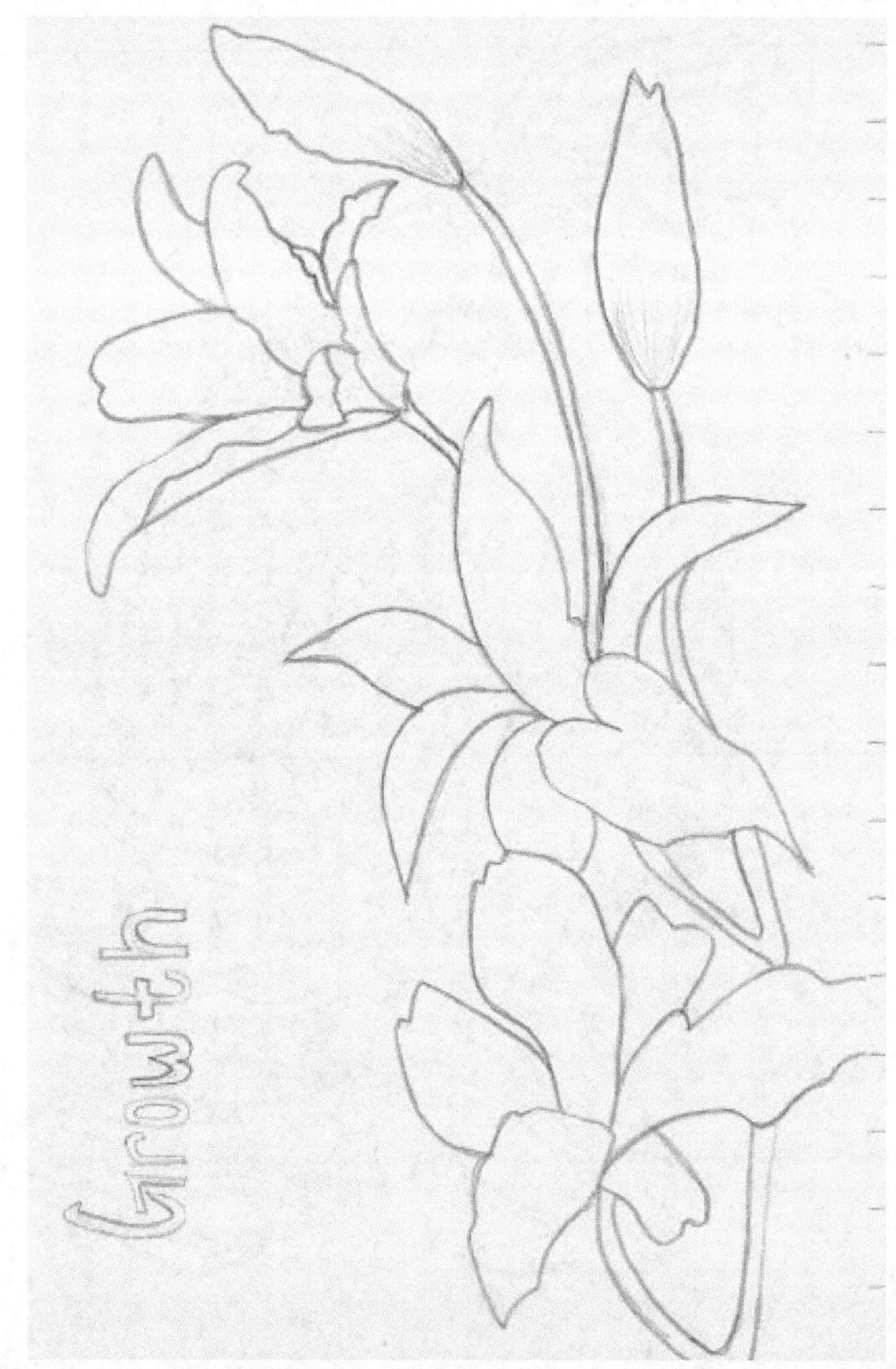

MY NOTES

MY NOTES

MY NOTES

MY NOTES

MY NOTES

MY NOTES

MY NOTES

MY NOTES

MY NOTES

MY NOTES

MY NOTES

MY NOTES

MY NOTES

My Notes

Don't be like the rest of them, darling   -Coco Chanel

My Notes

My Notes

My Notes

My Notes

My Notes

My Notes

My Notes

My Notes

My Notes

MY NOTES

MY NOTES

MY NOTES

MY NOTES

MY NOTES

MY NOTES

MY NOTES

MY NOTES

MY NOTES

MY NOTES

MY NOTES

MY NOTES

www.ingramcontent.com/pod-product-compliance
Lightning Source LLC
Chambersburg PA
CBHW081408080526
44589CB00016B/2495